FOUR EYES

FOUR EYES

STEVE BENSON

CITY POINT PRESS

Paperback ISBN: 978-1-947951-83-9
eBook ISBN: 978-1-947951-84-6

First edition

Published by City Point Press
www.citypointpress.com
Distributed by Simon and Schuster
For sales inquiries, contact Simon & Schuster (866) 506-1949
For rights inquiries, contact City Point Press (203) 349-8413

Manufactured in the United States of America

This book is dedicated to dear friends, Barrett, Carla, Kit, and Lyn.

ENTER

When you and I are kind to one another
  the war ends

Once you and I are
  kind to each other
  the warring ends
Once
  you and I were kind to each other
  as the war ended
Once you and I are kind to each other
  the war will be over

One time you
  were kind to me and the war ended
Once in my imagination
  the war was stopping kindness
  from reaching its ends
One war was stopping kindness
  from reaching

One warm foot was reaching out

One warm footing was reaching out

One warm foot was facing
  out
One way of facing out
  is finding a war raging
  inside you
One way you can face

When you and I are kind
  to one another the war
  ends
Once you and I are kind
  to each other the
  warring ends
Once you and I were
  kind to each othe4r as
  the war ended
Once you and I are kind
  to each other the war
  ends
Once you were kindness
  and the warring ends
Once in my image the
  was stopping kindness
  from reachsing an end
One war was stopping a
  kind person from each
  reach out
One warm foot was
  reality outside itself
One warm footing was
  resting on the ground
One wan face was
  feeling out the face
One way of feeling was
  finding a raging in your
  heart
One wisdom can feel its

away is inside you
One way I felt my brain swaying was
  inside you

One day I felt the rain
  make its way inside you
One day I felt the rain shape
  around us
One waving mane of
  unreal grains vegetables and fruits
  staged for pretended eating

One
  inside
  the day
  I felt her
  feeling a reach in toward her
One felt a reach in to
  the person inside
One was
  a face feeling out
  in the darkness

Once in the world
  of darkness that slid open
  that face emerged into light

That face merged into the light
  around it
That face felt itself
  merging into the light around it

The face felt an emerging light

way is inside
One wave I feel my
  brain sway was inside
  myself
One day I felt the rain
  making way inside us
One dame felt feels a
  shape around us
One waving maine of
  plastic grain staged for
  predtense of
  consummation
One inside the day once
  inside the person who
  was her felt herself
  feeling a reach in to her
  heart
One felt a reason in the
  self personhood feeling
One was felt a feeling a
  feeling a face outside
  the in the work of
  darkening
One in a world of
  darkeneing that slid that
  sliding face emerged
  into light
That face merged in the
  light face around it
The face felt merging
  into the face around the
  light
The face felt

around its feeling

The face no one could see
  was feeling itself
  finding out
  a merger   a merged state
In this emergency
  the feeling tone is rhyming
  opening out and unspooling

In the darkening that's gathering
  the faces feel

As if they themselves are becoming
  a mere register
  of what it means to be alive
Whatever it takes
  to be alive
  might mean taking
  another life
  back
One might mean to be taking
  another one away
  in one's imagination

One might make another meaning
  face into the light
  of one's
  feeling it out
Once one feels its light leaking out
  it feels fine
  like mist
One has missed oneself sometimes

an emerngency around it
feeling faces
The face no one could be
  was it   itself find out a
  merger of itself and
  another
It is an emergency the
  feeling tonight is
  reeling open into the
  night
In the dark the gathering
  faces the the feeling as
  of itse;lf
As if they were being a
  merger registration of
  faceness
Of whatever means it
  take be alive my
  meaning taking off
  another life beside
  onself
One might mean to be
  taking another one
  away in image of the
  face
One might make another
  meaning face into the
  imagine imaging
  feeling it there
Ononce feels its leaving
  it feels fine likke a
  missed ones
One has oneself once in

3

and in the darkness one might
maybe
find feeling opening up
One might feel one self
reeling open
seeming
what one seems to say

Once what one said
was always heard
one could always listen in
through a device
One could lean in to the device
and believe in it

Once listening to the device
I leaned in
and waved at myself

Once in a while
I could breathe

Once   in a while
I could breathe in
the idea
I could breathe the idea into the feeling

A feeling of feeling of thinking
if only out loud through the breathing

If I could feel what breathing
felt like

a time of darkness of maybe
one might or may not
find feeling opening up
One might feel oneself
reeling unrevaeling
seeming and seeing
what once said was
heard

Once what one said
saying was heardf once
always in to intself
through
Once could leave in the
device and leave in it
there listening

Once listening the the
device I listened in and
toward myself at
myself at myself

Once in a white time I
could become breathing
inside the device

Once in the device I
could breathe out the
feeling
I could brfeathe idea into
the feeling of thinking
aloud

Of a feeling out thinking
if only out loud through
the breath

Of I could feel what
bearthing dfelt in the

in that minute
because it felt
like my beating heart

My heart was beating
  inside my breathing
And one of us was being
  kind of alert
  and noticing
  what was sought to be thought there

One of us was sighing
  the same time as the other one
  thought about the sigh

One of us cried in a sign of
  thinking
  just barely
One of the times that we fell
  and the breath blew open the window
  through which I left

One time in the autumn
  I was there
  leaving as you entered

I was not leaving you
  but the space that was not there
  after you came in

One time after you found
  my belongings

lake breathing beside
myself felt my own
heart
My breathing breating
  my heart inside and
  being there too
And one of us what
  being kind of aware
  ande thinking and not
  thinking and was a sigh
  signed there
One of us was sighing
  the same time as the
  other one thinking
  sighed
One of of us cried in a
  sign of thin thought
  bare leaves thinning out
One of the in the fall the
  wind blew the leave the
  door opeened the leaves
  to fall
One time in the the
  autumn I was there
  leaving as you were
  e3ntering what
  became of us
I was wasn't leaving you
  but the space that was
  not there atfer you
  came in before me
Oned time ofater yuou
  find my belongings

left behind
I became a sign
One left one's belongings
 to become a sign
One left oneself in another body
 to become what was signed there

One had left and feeling what was left
 had opened the door
 to befriend what could be there

One was not myself
 but being there
 I could believe
I once thought I was being
 believing a signature
 when in eighth grade
I was signing everything
 with my signature then
I was belonging in the world
 of my signature
 there
In eighth grade where
 my signature belonged
 becoming looser and more open
In eighth grade where my
 signature became a sign
 of what would become
 and how I would belong
I would become
 a belonging
 to myself

leave you behind I
 became a sign
One left belong behind to
 be what was a sign
One left oneself in a sign
 to become was a body
 in mind
One had felt and feeling
 the last one there had
 opened what was to
 becoming
One was not me myself
 but becoming mnyself I
 could be leaving too
I once thought I was be a
 believing a signature
 whaten in 8th grade
I was signing every name
 with my signature then
I was beyound myself in
 the whirl of my
 signature there
In eighth grade whaere my
 signature belonged becoming
 looser and more open
In 8th grade where my
 signature became a sign
 of what I would
 become and beliong to
I would become
 recovered a beloonging
 to my own past and
 memory

I would become
  my past memory
  to enter the future

I would enter the future
  of my believings

  before it was too late

Before I left it was late   and I was too
I was left too
  and it was too late not to be so
I was left and left to it
  by myself there and so
I wanted to leave myself
  there in the scene
  we had shared
I wanted to be left there
  in the scene we had
  shared kindly together

I wanted never to leave
  that I had not had that kindness

I wanted a kind of feeling
  everything together
  together with you
I wanted my own kind of feeling
  with you too
  feeling it with me
I wanted what I won to be
  your winning too
I was seeing what I was feeling

I would become bettetr
  than my past of
  memory to enter the
  future
I would enter the future
  memory of the belives
  what I left beind

Beofre I lfeft It was late
  and I was too
I was left too and it wsas
  too late late not to be so
I tool was left and left to
  be myself there and so
I wantged to believe
  myself in there in the
  scene we had shared
I wanted to bereft there
  in the seeing we had
  shared kindness in
  together
 I wanted never to believe
  I had to leave that kind
  mess with you

I wanted a kind of messy
  everyhting together
  with you
I won my own kind of
  feeling with you too
  feeling your own too
I want what was I own to
  be your own won tune
 I wwas seeing what I was

as yours
and then I grew
I was seeing what
I felt there with you
grow
I was seeing
a feeling growing there
between us
I felt my own self
writing as I grew
to become more there
and feel all of you
I was feeling
what I knew was not you
in you there
I was my own feeling in myself
being what was not there
because it was you
So I was very much then
because I was being
I felt this in you
Because I was feeling myself
being there I felt in you a corresponding
felt tone
I felt a tune with you
that was stirring

I felt the contact between us
and I felt here
far from you and yet close

I felt inside you with me
what was closed

feeling as yourself and
then I grew
I was was seeing what
eye felt there with you
grow
I was feelt was feeling
seen feeling groan there
between you and it
I was feel my groan and
writhing as gto be there
with you and all of you

I was wanted to feel what
I was knew was not you
in you there
I was was my own eye
feeling being what was
not being there was you
Very much then Because
I was not me I felt this
in you
Because I was fee3l
myself I in you a
responding feeling tune
I felt in tune with you the
was stirred by your
contact
I feel the contact between
our skins and hearing
and from you and yet
very close
I fit in with you with me
what was closed and

and opened
I felt with you
  what was closed opened
I felt what was closing opening

I felt up your close chest
  and felt up my feeling
  inside
I felt up in my chest and felt
  a feeling rub over you

I felt felt over my chest
  feeling the rubbing of you

I felt rubbing again by you

I   well   I   made feeling
  and I became
  it too
I came to feel you
  and you did too
  because you know you
I won what I knew
  and I knew you were feeling
  what you were   not me
We know what we know
  but that's not what I mean
It is not I that feels
  but my little mind
  that thinks it knows
The way that thinks
  its knowing is fine and misty tonight

opened
I felt with you what
  closed opened
I feel what closes up
  opening up
I felt up your close chest
  and felt up my feeling
  inside
I felt up in my chest and
  felt a feeling rub over
  you
I felt felt over my chest
  feeling the rubbing of
  you
I felt rubbed against my
  you
I fwell I may feel it and I
  being came too

I came to you fear and
  you did too because
  you are not you
I wanted what I wanted
  to know in feeling and
  not me too
I and you feel what when
  why we no not that's it
Iit isn't what I that feels
  but my little eye that
  knows it
The where that thinks it's
  snowing is fine and
  misty tonight

It's finding mist in this night
  outside and inside of me

It's fine and I find it
  and it's missed and it's mine

It's whatever I did
  miss being here
  its being here tonight
In this I am not missing
  what I am meaning
  or its not being so true
And if I were ever true to you

  I would be belonging
I wonder how I would
  be in belonging here with you

In so doing
  I would be becoming you
  not really
I could not really
  become what you belong to

But in the night as I was saying
  I wanted to feel that mist on my face
  cold and wet
Its cold wet damp feeling
  was hitting me like a hard rock in the face
It was a hard rock
  that we felt through the glass
  that we were drinking from

It's finding mist in the
  night outside in inside
  of this here

It's fine and I find
  missing and mine
  tonight
It's whatever I didn't
  miss being is this in
  here is tonight
In this I am not missing
  what I meant I mean
  being so true to you
Iand if ever true if ever I
  were turuly tuning in to
  you belonging here
I wonder and hoe who I
  would be in being you
  inside
I in si the so it in this is
  be becoming you not
  real
I would would not not
  really belonging there
  with that
But in this night I was
  sne I want y cold and
  wet feeling
Its cold wet harsh dirty
  felt stone faced there
It was a hard a rock that
  we felt through the
  stein the drink came
  intto

When we drank it was not over yet
  It was hard to get over it

It was hardly over yet it was
  something still
  and we were inside it
It was drinking from us
  where we stood
  and we were feeling a longing
  as if we were somewhere else
It was there that we
  drank that nectar of forgetfulness
  that we had longed for

It was in that lengthy shot
  of dark mist
  that we felt
  around for our feeling wants

Inside that dark mist
  of the clothes that had gotten soggy out
  there we felt our brains tingle as the air
  hit them
As the air hit us on our clothing
  that was wet and shivering
  we felt ourselves
  in our faces
Whenever we felt the rain
  sizzling across
  our terrain
  we felt the names of
  a wildness   and our voices became hoarse
Our hoarse breath

I want to drink It was not
  yet of it hard to get
  over
It was hardly over yet it
  wa a still drinking it

It drank from our lips
  where stoanding belong
  for not being there

It wasn't there that we
  drank that need to
  forgetfulness that that
  we lengtheend
I t was in that lengthy
  shower of dark
  messiness that we felt
  around for our longing
  what was there

Inside that darkaness of
  damp closing up we
  soggy rains tingle as air
  faired well
As the air hit us acorss
  on clothes wet and
  simmering we spelt our
  names erased
Wehenever we felt the
  rain sizzling acorss our
  shifting terrible strain
  we felt a mane of a
  wild hoarse breathing
Out hoarse breathe

breathing in and out
after hours and hours of
believing we were there
we felt that we could breathe in that air

We are now not kind
and wet but we are
where we belong
We came along from
the dark places we couldn't see
in our imaginations
and we left behind
our warm
hot breath

breathing in and out
and hours and hours
believing we were not
only there but beliong
in that air
We are not anow naughty
and yet but we are
where we began
We can out and from the
darkness we could only
see in our images or
signs   and we left
behind out warm hot
breaths

TRANSRELAFLECTIONS

I am reminded of—

Well, I don't know where this came from.

I had imagined this all going some other way.

I had imagined it differently before.

If you had been there, it was about four or five months ago,

the clouds were gently undulating like this up in the sky—

but there was no movement to them at all, except of course there was

but you can't see it, because you're in a different kind of time. . . .

Do you think it's entropy that's working that way?

—when your time goes differently than that of another person

or the natural world

or whatever   you might be thinking of   at the time

Who is here?
Wer ist da?
Where are you?

There are all these interruptions, anyway,   and they're elastic, too

The interruptions themselves could have interminable depth and strenuous force

They could meet you half-way, if you happen to walk in the right direction,
Wenn Du in die richtige Richtung läufst
and sometimes you can't know in advance what the right direction

is going to be, because you're stumbling away from that

durable, penetrating pressure, and yet the next thing that you know

you've walked right into it, like a log that

— trip over — the little pieces you know that stick out of the log

that scratch your leg if you're not wearing insulating federal trousers
…die Dein Bein zerkratzen wenn Du keine….
—is that what they call them now?— to make sure that no stains are left

by the blood that seeps off the surface of your skin

as something has slipped in there. . . .
…irgendwas ist hier reingerutscht und –
Excuse me.

Wait!!   Oh yeah, I missed the bus again.

It was so enabling to be caricatured in such a surprising way

I didn't think of it backwards like that

I was just an indentured servant, I suppose, doing my best . . .
Ich hab nich' rückwärts darüber nachgedacht
Well, slip me a Mickey, please.

I've been here before, I can feel it now. It's—

Ich war hier schonmal, ich weiss es ganz genau – ich spür's…

That's probably why, why I brought these notes.

Deshalb hab ich die wahrscheinlich mitgebracht

For context!!   . . . and . . .   [laughing] What's the difference between concept

and . . . no, no, that's the wrong word.   [snaps fingers]

…das ist definitiv das falsche Wort!

"Without reflecting. Are you listening? And so, what is there to be said?

Crowds, old times, memories. The bright screen

thrown into obscurity by the page increasingly dot dot dot dot

…punkt, punkt, punkt, punkt…

like vines on the white painted brick"   Some people have to go under the table

[crawling and crouching under a conference room table]   This is how it is—

it's like this—   It's not that unusual really to spend hours like this,
Manchmal sollte man einfach unter den Tisch gehen – s' is' nich' so ungewöhnlich!
and then, hopefully there's somebody really nice. . . .   [re-emerging to stand].

And, they—don't you—I wonder if Bob Dylan's looking out the window down the street

and he sees somebody walking like this, does he think,

"That could have been me"?   Probably.
Könnte das ich gewesen sein? Denkt der das könnte ich gewesen sein? Wahrscheinlich.
He would. It's— Overnight —

Gosh, it changes so much from minute to minute.   Overnight, there's a ballpark
Gott das verändert so viel!
where there's— a game is playing— you can see it from the rooftop at night—

huge cheering and shouting of everybody in there, they're very excited.   And when

there's a baseball game, there's always two teams. One of them wins and one of them

 loses.   [handing cards to the other speaker]
          S'sind immer zwei Teams – eins gewinnt, eins verliert.
        And if you're not there,   it doesn't make too much sense.
[who passes cards out to the people]   Wenn Du nich' da bist macht's nicht
                Now, when you get the cards, you can hold them, or put them down.
allzu viel Sinn…
You can distribute them further, if you like – everybody could pass the card that they've

got to their right.
                    Jeder kann seine Karte nach rechts weitergeben.
You could pass it to the right again, you could pass it to the left.
      Du kannst's auch

                                        It's –
wieder nach rechts geben, oder auch nach links weitergeben.
                              The cards are for you.

You could pass them out to the other people, nearby.
              Die Karten sind für Euch.

Aber ihr könnt sie auch andern weitergeben.
But don't forget what's written on your card. *[audience laughter]*
                          Aber vergesst nicht was auf Eurer Karte steht!
        The space is elastic.   It tends to move.

When there's pressure put against the edges of the space, sometimes it crumples

  and buckles.   When the wind blows too hard on the space,

the people in the space   fly into pieces,   their arms splayed out

...im Raum zerfallen sie in Stücke –

[stretching arms straight up and out]   in a violent *curve*, like that.

They don't know what's on their minds anymore,

and they're infiltrated by dreadful thoughts from advertising
                              ...sie wissen nicht mehr worüber sie
all around the edges of the environment.   The edges of the environment
nachgedacht haben...
constantly creeping closer and closer, the same way that the clouds don't move.

You see them in your skin with the pores that have become sensors in your body

because your eyes don't function anymore.

So, this is a very uncomfortable situation.
                                        Ziemlich unangenehme Situation!
        You can have a handle for it, if you like,

at considerable cost.   It's possible to raise the money, though,

because there are *endless*—just so many *resources in this world,*

if you just know how to *grab onto them.*

It's like the thing about the chair, right?   Some people know how to lift the chair

with one hand so it doesn't seem to tip over at all,
                Manche Leute können den Stuhl
You can do that.   You can do that.
 mit einer Hand hoch heben; fällt nicht um –
Yeah, it's said that this kind of behavior,   this kind of measured,

gently, — auggh! - - - - - this, this this this creeping inwardness ... could be, in itself,

if administered to someone who's unwilling, it could be torture, of a sort.

Man könnte das auch Folter nennen – auf die ein- oder andere Art und Weise.
And the ...   So, there are tortures that work, and tortures that don't work.

Mache Foltern funktionieren und manche nicht.
We've been encouraged to apply the tortures that don't work, in order to learn more

  from our environment. Unfortunately, we're getting into a really stinky mess.

So I would think that   releasing pressure would be good.   And indecipherable
                    S'wär ganz gut ein bisschen Druck loszuwerden ...
information   might be one way to do that.   But—

But this is something that we don't know how to accomplish now.

We're breathing in and we're breathing out.
                                        Wir atmen ein, wir atmen aus.
We're checking our watches.
                        Wir gucken auf die Uhr.
We're verifying the schedule.
                          Bestätigen den Stundenplan...
  Insisting on what we don't know . . . .

And the *sugar* on the *pill* is frozen there,

so that when you put it in your mouth it sticks to the surface of your tongue.

You can't breathe anymore.

[opening laptop preset facing the group, in front of the podium, pressing buttons,

until the sound comes on]   You're like the slot machine so jammed up with quarters

 and whatever people put in them these days   that there's no more movement

in the energies anymore at all.

Keine Bewegung mehr in den Energien.

And your experience is one of media sliding across place with itself, with each other.

[*computer bleep*] The edge of that is tucked in to the other side, where the head is loose.

He was able to adopt a kind of theater about himself. Actually, the very first time

that I met him, he was really acting, in a way. And that was good because you can go

anywhere when you're somebody else. Cinderella, she seems so easy. 'It takes one to

know one,' she smiles. *Uaunghh!!* [shaking the shut laptop in the air at arm's length,

gasping]   [*bleep*]   The simple thing is that

you can do it *too*—you just take the threads out, one at a time, one at a time,
einen Faden nach dem
and each of your socks could become kind of a new   experiential surface for you.
anderen rausziehen…   und jede von Deinen Socken könnte was Neues –

                          eine Experimentierfläche werden für –
It's not hard   to make   of   that –
       Es ist nicht schwierig!
what was containing you could become   something that you hold . . .

           in embarrassment.   We throw around these words.

They could enable us to perceive other, other formulas.

You can hand in your cards at any time. The end is like a rush

where everybody is hurrying all at once to the same place at the same time.

Am Schluss sind alle in Eile

They never make it because you can't coincide with another person

und versuchen irgendwie an den gleichen Ort zu kommen – das kannst Du aber nicht

per-per-per-per- perpendicularly in time and space.

schaffen! –

You have to create a role for yourself,

you have to imagine and invent a space in which you can inhabit the castle

that the dawn is folding itself up on either side, until the wiggle room breaks wind

and the tossed and turning atmosphere is struggling to embarrass *itself*—

It is no longer ashamed of you or me. It's no longer siphoned off

like the oxygen or carbons, all the materials that make air

All' die Materialien die Luft –

pregnable and livable, that make us — ability to suffer in one dimension —

replicable. And so instead there's this coming into the center of everything.

Stattdessen kommt es ins Zentrum von Allem.

It's partly knots,

and it partly could be anything,

Teilweise könnte es Alles sein.

so you just investigate at your own risk, really.

No one's going to believe you anyway,

                         S'wird Dir sowieso niemand glauben!

but there's a purpose to it, which is to set an example.

Because people are watching, actually, people are always watching,

S'schaut immer irgend jemand zu

and they're *confused*, in fact, though seldom as aware of their confusion

as you feel as you're trying to do the right thing in their—

                           meistens sind sie sich nicht bewusst,

dass sie so durch'nander sind wie wir, wenn wir versuchen das Richtige zu machen

well, not in their name, because you can't really do that,

                            aber nich' in ihrem Namen –

         it would be kind of preposterous, um . . .   [finger snapping]

s' kannst Du nicht machen –

What's the word?   Yeah – words, exactly.   If you had the right words,

       Was war das Wort?

you could probably build a bridge all the way from here to —

         Wenn Du das richtige Wort hättest könntest Du wahrscheinlich

       There's a village on the hill that's probably in the shape of

ne Brücke bauen

       an *old* thermometer, filled with mercury, sort of tilted up, like that,

so that everybody could see it but from a different angle it looks different.

Thank you. My hand writing.   At first the word looks like handwriting.

       Meine Handschrift –

Then you back up and you come back in towards it and you realize that

erst sehn' die Wörter wie Handschrift aus.

it's saying something to you.

       Dann gehst Du ein Stück zurück und Du merkst –

In this case, it's giving me ideas,

it's giving me ideas about coming into being in some way. And I don't know

what the ideas are, because I don't understand the language. But it's stressing

(in a nice sense) the possibility of becoming someone more than just myself—

in other words, well, you know, *why don't we all*— you know, if I—

No, it's so much simpler than that, because it's happening all the time anyway—
Es ist so einfach!
If I just become steeped in—stepped into—well, be—being one, with— hmm,

Eins sein mit – hmm…
myself?— *I* can— It's— There's no distinction any longer between me and you,

it's patently clear.
S'gibt keinen Unterschied mehr zwischen mehr Dir und mir-
So, [big yawn and stretch]
ist ja klar!
whenever you do get, you know, bored and tired of living, think again.

Because there are always other people around, mattering, just as much as you do,
Es sind immer andere Leute da
maybe more,   in their way.   And that's quite a bit to be grateful for.
die genauso wichtig sind wie Du.
Now I just had one or two more things

that I wanted to say—
Ich will nur noch ein oder zwei Sachen sagen.
Because, in all the exhaustion and all the *slippage* that of course happens

as we pick one thing up and it turns into another thing and we—   we—

A fantasy of who I'm going to be

with somebody else and who somebody else is going to be with me

                    Eine Phantasie wer ich sein könnte mit jemand anderem
  erodes by all the friction against the reality of time moving through space
und wer der andere mit mir sein könnte
as it inevitably does. It's like a—   it's a whole lost art really.

You can do it too!   In the end, I keep saying— I keep sane that way.   That's it.

Ahh.   But, me too.
        Hmmm...
It's a gift to me that you were able to pay any attention to me at all today.

   And I wish to give you the same, one of these times.

[alarm beeping]   Thank you.

ORATION AT BERKELEY

I want to thank you for a wonderful introduction, I really appreciate it a lot, and
    very generous and thoughtful, and we've been having a really terrific conference here
that has been going on yesterday and today, and began an elaborate conversation that has involved
both the keynote speakers and the performers the organizers
various persons who have been respondents to the keynote speakers
and it's really been fabulously interesting and exhibited a lot of energy
So my interest tonight is to somehow respond to what we've been able to do in the last few days and those of you
who've seen or participated in parts of it will appreciate that, I'm sure

There, you can hear, a sound, in the background, of somebody working on a typewriter
    It sounds like it's across the street or down the alley but you can't quite hear it exactly
        It's in the middle distance   and people are talking as they pass
        and the earth is made of concrete around—and tarmac   so the airplanes lift off
        and there's a bleak horizon in the middle distance
        and the sky is arcing overhead
        and the people are spitting out the windows of the plane because air pressure is very low
        and then they're trying to increase air pressure by releasing fluids into the outer air
as they've been receiving instructions from the pilot but they receive them in a kind of garbled fashion
    because the sound system is defective or perhaps it's intentionally designed to blur things

so as people get more excited and spit harder

Nobody knows for sure

But I know what I've seen, and it's elastic and formulaic

So, to begin again, I place myself in these hands of

escalating situations   We slip ahead into the foreground

People are there and they are wearing waffles as a kind of clothes

They're stitched together with noodles, soft noodles but they get hard overnight

and that's where people usually wear them, is to bed

because that's the most comfortable place if you're wearing something that embarrassing

You usually try to lie very still on your back or on your front

because if you lie on your side you're going to start cracking the waffle open

and you get colder—it's not alright

So, like I say, people are there, and they're coming—they're coming closer all the time

and they have personal problems and they have conditions in their lives that we don't know about

so there's a design problem   but they don't know about that either

Their level of stress is interminable and un-determinable, and it's fortunate that they're moving

They're always moving in time, but you can't see that, because they're in another spot

Their zone is masked from your zone, but it's possible that

there are devices to get there, there might be Energy Theory for example

If everything is reduced to molecules, then all the molecules are metaphorical

and the metaphors are *diced*—they grow organically, as dice, six-sided and eight-sided, alternating

as they appear, so that you can roll them and throw them and you can tumble with them

It's recommended that you try to become human dice, because then you can understand how they're experiencing

their resolutions of their own quandaries, their own uncertainties, their own difference

becomes your difference.   And so, you can handle that.   It's like a role—

      it's not a breakfast roll, it's a tumbling roll like that

    You didn't think you could do it but there you did it!   Perfectly!

And the body is streaming on ahead

So, we've been here, and other people have been in other places

    and some of them have been typing on typewriters

    and some of them have been mounting and descending vehicles of transportation

    and some of them have been imagined and some of them have been imaginary

    but the time has been shifting so that we can read our memories through them

So,   in the beginning, we thought about how best to put our minds together and become a bubble

      that had many sides, as many sides as there are molecules to the bubble

      and each molecule had several sides as well

      and the molecules themselves were spinning and rubbing together

    There was a lubricity and a quality of unpronounceable energy to them

    that was changing their design   and you could see them together that way

But overnight we lost touch with the enemy and there was a gigantic ursine creature

that *attacked* suddenly from the basement, where they were square-dancing and they didn't know

that their revolutions and boundaries were collapsing into the form of a *gigantic bear*

    It was like three feet high, and no one could see it but it was descending rapidly from the skylights

      until, washed out and threadbare, it scuttled across the floor

A crab developed an itch. A square dance hinged on a negative tripod. You had belief in your back pocket
and it was black—your pocket was covered with inky film that couldn't, couldn't come off on your hands
        It was a mysterious miracle, because you knew that you could never wear these pants again
        but you could still feel your hands on your face, you could still find the threads on your chest
        and you could still sense the potential in your body for release of tension
                for freedom, exercise of sexual and sensual satisfactions
                and there was a brightness in the shadow that was cast

        behind your back—Now when I say "you" I don't necessarily mean you as an individual person
        or anybody that you know. I speak *generatively* in order to *propose* a you that you are free to become
                and you can choose to do that at any moment, preferably the moment of change . . .

        Change   into   fresh   accent   Monitor   safe   turns

We might be thinking about what being used to being used in poetry means
Supposing there are actions that ideas that seem the best are put intricately well into an ink-well
and pulled out, like a pair of second-hand pants. There's a dialogue between materials here
so that what is known and what is noticed have a constant interplay, but they're unstable—
constantly expanding into a fable of lies as life is rigorously unoccupied by hesitation or murder
        The answer to a sore drum feels fancy and funnily furious, faked, and it finds itself in tones
        It finds itself in an asterisk that creates a form, a form creates an answer
In the work of an absorbed Martian intelligence, there elides fantasy and corporeality, a structure of internalized
invention that plays with vital facts and forces to become elephants for a day
        It's called Elephant Day, and it happens once every year. *You can wear gray on Elephant Day!*
        And that's where your fantasy will coincide with the force of a shared understanding

27

a solitary introspective moment that doesn't make your sense sensational

It doesn't squeeze an aspect of meaning into a form that the world can register without you

      You have to believe in the internal budget, a bucket of tumbling oxygen oxides

They threaten to strangle you from the inside, but you are already inside out, so it doesn't matter

I'm reminding you that I'm positing a you—   You is a theoretical construct in this case

so not to be implied, or specified, other than as   a form of possibility

You can ruin yourselves running

Your cells run down and become battered by adversity, interchange

icons roaming through a *forest* or a *form* of seldom slanted lies

The lines become piddling, driven by sneak previews

      The program is truth, and truth is harmonically mystified

I was speaking earlier about the budget. The budget is very wide, and slow, so you can rest and relax in it and it rolls over hills and down into valleys. It soothes itself on form and creates non-form by its slippery investigation of form – "slippery" in the sense of being cast in a dream world, an impenetrable fortress of personality, specious and logical and sincere at the same time. Its answer is frozen as an icon, switched on by an avatar in a skilled replication of unanswered cell-phones. Its purpose is to be haunted. Its name is ungovernable. Its sweltering heat is a reminder of the distant past.

People are hard at work, and their forms are   tilted by the mode of reproduction

They can't see how much they're wrestling with, so they sleep in a shadow that's cast before all other things whereas they seem stuck in a kind of gluey elusive luminosity   cancelling each other out

It's a skid, such as one might mount furniture or bales of cartoons upon   an aspect of fumbling insecurity

shamed or shaved or erased by interminable specious

Swivel back. *The course has been run!* You can answer the blade

You can be be be be be be be be be be be be *betray your owner.* Your boss is forgiven

frustrated and *impervious to exercise muscles, exercise muscles!* Profoundly

raped by code, by misused *word language and images too*   It's *the wrong word!*

So that's when the bell peals off

the label, and when that happens, there's a, it's more than, it's like a gigantic rupture

in the surface of the container so that everything that's inside of it whatever that might be goes *rushing out*

into the surrounding atmosphere   People don't know what to do

The nature of that is virtually impossible to specify but it does answer an experience

an experience that was propped up and shot out and overnight the attention was or–orashe-or-orat-

oratic!

Attention had a warm, fierce, lightning glow about it that attracted everybody's indifference

They were astonished by how little they cared about anything suddenly

They couldn't think for wondering how they got there and what I am *mean!*

Their senses were all stirred up until they lost their *grip* and their *slipped* and they *sloshed*

and their legs went over their heads and their feet fell off their all their legs and arms slipped and slided

and the water was *craning and crashing* and everything was *so slow* that it was *violent* and it was excited

and people were dusting themselves off, and *another one came*

and then people were tripping over themselves trying to get there first

Nobody had a rigid idea about it   People only had plastic ideas
          ideas that could change form and shape under the influence of each other's ideas
So everybody was like sharing their ideas back and forth
          and some people's different ideas started like looking like looking like different things
          and but that was beside the point—it didn't matter what they *looked* like
          it was what they *acted* like that mattered, so it might be looking like a flying pig
but it would *act* like a brontosaurus in *heat*, and it was *scary* to those other ones who acted like
          little first graders who just wanted to find the right way to dot their i's or cross their t's
          or answer the telephone or maybe they would like to become novelists or dramatists, dramaturges
          they might like to run a theater of their own one day and put on plays of Ibsen or Chekov
But, when you feel like you've been framed, there's   there's
                              an uncaring swerving path through the garden
          so that the garden is growing and the planets are stirring there
                    creating germinal   experiences of foraged contention
          They're bashing and battering each other in order to make difference
          and difference is conclusive in a way that has absolutely no credibility
          so you are always sharing the team or scene with a displaced hierarchy
          a hierarchy that is turned to flow in a flux and that the angle at which it hits is bright and starlit
                    and there's no purpose to this relentless remorseless transit
We were relying on an underlying   ball, ball game, a bald plane on which things rested and rolled
          shimmered and thought they were taut but they were loose and skirmishing in the brushes
          that fired the distant hills into still bright beacons
beacons that shifted to icons when they were still

In *viewing an image of a reading matter*, there's always a difference and . . .

this thing is a book. The book has a left page and a right page

The right page is obscured by another illustration

Actually a letter, *a page of a letter*, not the full letter

a page of a letter from the author to the reader of the book

The book is heavy but not very heavy, so that the hand is cupping the book to hold it up

and the writing here is written by hand but the writing here is written by some unknown

cultural creation, a technological uniformity, which makes it   *easy to read*

but it once it had something to do with this other hand

not this hand, which is very big, but this empty space complements this space

which is mostly empty but it has a text in it

So if you look at the page there's a text in it and it's all over here near the middle of the gutter

and this refers to books, you can see

This page is not empty, and it has something else that was done by hand, but not really, on here

This is an imitation, but this one over here was done with another hand, but this was written on purpose

And this is another hand, this is not the mirror of this, it's a residue

Like this picture here, you can see there's a picture here too, but it's not the same picture as here

And there's always a picture so on this page this is the picture for this text and this is the picture for this text

and the space around them is flowing and creating movement around the text so that you can see it

as a text that's in motion as well as that it can breathe while it moves

And some of the text again becomes like an indicator of no text

And sometimes a text can be an illustration as here, one text is a picture of the other text but it's not the same text, and that, this text illustrates this text, but also this text illustrates *this* text depending on which text you're interested in at the time, and so

but the picture that's created by this text is a sound picture and this text creates a sound picture and they reflect each other in that way but whether this text has a meaning picture that's the same as that is entirely contestable because everyone will read it in a different way and what you see won't be the same

So what's around and outside of what you see is also always a part of the text

If you're only looking at one page then the rest of the image of your viewing field, what you see peripherally could be as easily just part of what's in the text

So that here we see the page of the book that's written and printed, and it's being held by the hand and it's on another book, which has this fake picture on it, which is being held by

The book is being held by the hand that is holding the picture that has words on it that look like they're printed by a machine or a logical intelligence

but really they're created by writing or drawing

by this same, no, this same hand here, and it's a memory picture

This is a non-memory picture. I don't know what to make—I mean non-memory— each of these pictures here, I don't remember anything about them except not understanding them before even though it presents clear labels for each

I think this kind of text is *really* difficult to understand of the pictures

but it's like looking at graphs, I never know how to I have to stop and think really hard and the little dots over here you could see These'll probably to fill in the answers

And this page shows what books look like when they have interesting pictures that complement the writing so that again there's a quality of peripheral looking so that you're looking at something and they're reading something but it's not the same

and you get to go back and forth between looking at something that's not a bunch of words and

but in a picture book like this you're seeing a picture but you get to find out that there are these lines of

writing in it that are creating a picture that again has a kind of force and regularity and a strong making

meaning by making everything look the same and regular in a certain way, but then if you want to know

what the words are saying, it's a different kind of question

and there's a page that might be the same or there's a page that's blank

so that here, this page isn't a mirror of this page, and you might think it's an extension of it

but it's really on the other side of the visual field

And here on the other side of the visual field is a whiteness, an openness

that doesn't answer any questions   though you can see that it leads to something else, so that—that –

something else that you can't see   but you can almost imagine

something else that's pregnant and imaginable

And here you can see that there are shapes and lines that the artist who made the book has created

just as here you can see there shapes and lines in the background that are part of the page view

even though they're not part of what you see

And, as the words become close, if you put on your glasses and you peer really closely at it

or you get one of those special magnifying glasses you can see that something in the page

This is another memory picture, from a long time ago, a book by Walt Whitman

and the words are irregular, because they're very very old, and memory is fading out

as we look at the books and we see that sometimes one d doesn't look like another d because they're old

They're changing and decaying with time, but they're very sensual, they're very thick with *accrued* meaning

and value, because of all the time that they've lived together on the page and all the people who've
rubbed their eyes and imaginations against them, who've swung and rolled with them
who've kind of been swilled and sweated with them, and hurt with them
and released into surprising states of happiness or glow with them

So there's more than one sound in the air and there's more than one word on the page
and attention is constantly stretching and shifting in order to be aware of the different possibilities
of things that can move it on and ways that it can stretch to know about more than one thing
so that it's sweating and stirring and sweeping and sleeping and freezing and weeping and ssss-shifting
This clearly was written during war, war is referred to in this, or war is being remembered in the text
written when the place itself was stormed and disturbed, taken through hell by war
and then that piece of hope that people needed was cherished and worried over

The page over here is only partially visible and tilted   and this page is only the bottom part of the page
and the word 'taver' is only part of a word

So I want to see what can come   if I breathe gently   and say what I think is meaningful to me
The difference is perpetual   and it has a slippery edge   that is only   a sliding nocturnal wish
a wish to go where one is safe
a wish to behave and to sleep in a dream space
a special case and a way to be seen by that

Where   Where we went   Watched   Wells wash up   the shore bent and blended
stirred   seems the same   spurred, sparkled, turned

34

The appearance   turned and   the wondering learned what it needed to want   to know

how it could burn and sparkle   Shapes erupt while the universe slows down to a creak

and makes unmanageable time and place pieces collapse

Formulas enhanced by bracken and brickbat, by suds and solemnity, stew

stoop to learn what they need to share among the people who are ax-accetted by their glow, their nose

Technology is extremely valuable and unsafe   It creates misunderstandings and it presents

preliminary sweat-lodge boundaries   wedges of unpredicated smell factors and skinny robberies

slip storms   middle of the bend works   squashed smells   and bad black fame memories

It's a speech that is speaking and spurned, spurred on by the middle distance, by the range, the scope

What the, what the, what the rest arises is aroused by the mess, the special

frenzy of finding speculative intentness seems specious but not shown

to be alone, to be restless, to be rude   to be spooked even

What's, what's happened isn't real

The answer is surprising because it didn't exist before the question

Its vertical axis is crumbling

I don't believe this could be happening

But the matter made a mistake

It stirred up an impertinent probability

And that pattern was not of a matter of what I sss eyes ice over with thought blamed and blanked out

an interruption in un-stymied time but a blank nose swept over the entire surface to make

meaning swirl and congeal, to break up and force a field aside

TIME SQUARED

*I developed a curious practice in my moments of waiting to
which I gave the name of prayer, nondiscursive prayer. In the
blackness behind my closed eyeballs I projected a small square in
which were enclosed the words I was contemplating. For some
reason I still do not understand, the shape of a square served me
better than that of a circle or a triangle, although I tried out every
geometric shape I could conjure up. I then moved the words out
of the square, leaving blackness enclosed in blackness.*

—Doris Grumbach, *The Presence of Absence*,
page 18, Beacon Press, Boston, 1998.

I'm tired
I'm bushed
Feelings
Feeling I'm tired of looking
(The words are still only semi-audible)
Town
Sound grows on sand
Looking makes me tired
All these fashion monkeys everywhere I look
And then there's this other guy I run into in the mirror
He doesn't know what he's doing
Oh yes . . .
I'm tired of looking
Tired of looking
I'm tired of talking
I'm tired of listening,
I'm tired of hanging out
I'm tired of waiting

I'm tired of thinking so hard about it

I'm tired of being nervous

I'm tired of feeling tired

I'm getting bored

(Crowd noise is fading)

I'm very excited, actually, but my sister-in-law is here

and she just gave me this really intense look

and she doesn't know what's happening

because she's expecting something somebody else, a different brother in law,
    maybe, I don't know

So I'm

I'm just working it out, bit by bit, and, the oh yeah

So, and the baby wailed blue murder, and the sky turned velvety black, and
    pigment froze in my skin

The message was over complicated

The tiles shifted places

shifted the plates on the floor

were shifting erratically

dynamically, sporadically, spastically confected

A lot of time on-line buying a gift for her

I'm a busy guy

I work at a distance

in a room, far away from the shelves

bordered with little toy ducks and symbols that stand for a way of life that's
    become decrepit and outdated

There's plenty of room in the room but there's only so much room in the doorway

It's a little cold up here, but it will warm up after a while

because the windows might open after a while, and

and it's going to change season

It used to be November

It used to be December

It used to be January

There are more presidential campaigns to come

Somebody took my beer

The latte is delightful!

You don't need to scream to say that

It's not

It's not special

It's a special way to think

It's containments, containments

The times that, the times squared

What does that mean?

It's a mathematical term

When three or nine is time squared

It means that the ah

Metaphorically speaking it's like an umbrella opens but it's actually a globular world

the world round and becoming different than a

than it had been in your imagination

and your imagination's constantly *changing!*

So, it's a surprise, kind of an everyday sort of surprise that you don't expect to have
     happen, but it can happen, and, and, and there's plenty of seats over here, too

There's plenty of seats, and if anybody wants to sit down, let's see

There's a lot of room, and, uh, but

Big city, too

Big city and there's a lot of people who are looking for space

Not everybody has space

On the bus, I was asked

Where is the homeless shelter

because *I was one of the other people on the bus!!*

I wasn't the only person there

There were quite a few

and they didn't answer, so I had

I had the iPhone

and I looked up what I could

and I gave her an address

She had Jesus

statements on

around her neck

on threads or strings

or ribbons or rubber bands

encased in plastic, because it was a rainy day

She'd planned ahead

She knew what she was doing

She was looking for a homeless shelter

and I knew what she was doing cause she told me

It's hard to read upside down

Arm set the tamp tramp maybe? sailed

Yeah, the tramp sails at sunset

I remember writing that line

The one above it is, we, below it, from my point of view, is

We liked today so much, I think

On the phone

You can use the phone to bring things to you

these days

The phone'll do

bring things into focus, it says here

The words, the why-not, the donut, a question with an answer in it

embedded in it, right in the middle

like you

You can kind of poke it out with your thumb or something

There's not that much room in the doorway

but there's a lot of room in the room, and

It's free

People are encouraged to move around

The ceiling is completely open

No one has tried that yet at all

And the stairwell is really good if you like to be walking up and down while you're here

There's no law against it

It hasn't been deregulated yet

I mean re-regulated yet

but your behaviors in other place

I have no authority

I have no authority to *speak* about that

That's been regulated

Okay, after a.m., oh yeah, with Zeya, Iris and I drove to Castine to see Legos
    Robotics tournament Jasper worked on

Energy Piglets!

That was a good project.

12 10 07 11:47 p.m., Monday

Caroline and I met with Jasper's teachers to tell about, oh yeah, about changing
    over to the Bay School

Oh yeah, this is a long time ago

Ahh, 2007, we changed schools for him, and then I had a meeting with them, also
    about a client, also, because I was working with somebody else in the school

I had to meet with the teachers

Both were affecting

Jasper handled the announcement well

He didn't know this was about to happen, I guess

It was a long time ago and my memory is dim

Seemingly with quiet pleasure and no sign of disturbing regret

he said some of his friends will be mad

And it talks about playing games and stuff

So that's one side of the page is like that and the other side is like *this*

As the position you straddle it in

Vertigo increases with anxiety

Balancing ability predisposes one to seasickness

Am I on mic?

It's so mysterious in here

It's really great!

Acoustical preferences

I think of a room as having its preferences for acoustics

And this room really favors this

The acoustics in this rug here

They're very like soft and bouncy

It's really

If you want to listen well and you want to come over and put your head close to
the rug you're welcome to

Just don't step on my CDs

To be ***AGGHH!!!***

Oh I thought I was stepping on something important

It's my shoes

Did I break anything in anybody's eardrums?

Sorry

Wow, look, there's only one chair left!

They moved!

Oh thank you!

Uh, rage at client who has de—disec—desecrated Christmas tree

decorated Christmas tree with family at hour he scheduled my home visit for

Oh that's the bottom of the page

As the position you straddle it in, vertigo increases with anxiety

Balancing ability predisposes one to seasickness

One mariner explained

How do I come up with this stuff?

She still holds my thumb

in sleep

Angry

Preoccupied with my own needs

Really preferences

Self-righteous, almost moralistic

So what?!!

So what?!!

Again and again

I'm *breaking*

and trying to notice even the fact that I'm breathing

It all slows me down

So I want to fly

So I want to fly the words the why not the donut a question with an answer in it

You drink and feel your thirst

I believe we believe

There will be no tomorrow

We like today so much

The tramp sails at sunset

After the crowds disperse, the burden of sodden lies spread across the floor

You see it's the same thing in here

The sodden lie

You are not here

You are here

You understand everything, whether I say it or not

That word keeps cropping up

The origins of the word are cloudy, as is the weather

The day after tomorrow!

The whole earth rumbles rumbles rumbles so softly only you can feel it

It goes there

That down volume, down

Tomorrow tomorrow

Will this be typed?

7 03 07

I have this idea

that starting on July first

whenever I wrote in my journal on the left side

of the spread of two pages I would write poetry

something called poetry on the right right after that

It could be anything if I could remember

if I could remember

Oh yeah, the line breaks are sometimes not where I would put them

Uhh, did I ever turn that on?

And, Yeah!

Where I would put them

Where I would put them

Where I would put them
Physical body coming there
And I don't always
want to
Writing them, right from the left margin
here a natural law we know as human, a natural legacy, a
Ancestors, ghosts!
Ancestors are not ghosts
Ancestors are ghosts
To be speaking or not speaking
To know or to not know
To know or to not know
Not knowing and saying it
Saying
Saying that which I don't know
Saying it's so and makes it what
is still, still, silent, stuck
left sitting in the refrigerator while away on a trip and the power goes out in the
        middle of the winter in a heavy ice storm
There is nothing to do but complain inwardly
though outwardly I just look morose and hurt
Yes I hurt, listening
to sounds
I cannot interpret well enough
t*o know*
whether they are animal or human or just my own body
body echoing chaotically
because I'm so tired!
My teeth fell out
and maybe sickly
That would lead to
You see if your teeth, if you have a really big problem with your teeth, you'll have
        cavities and uh, and then your cavities will affect your nervous system, and
        eventually your brain will decompose, so brush

Well, when you do brush

You don't need to brush regularly, but if you don't brush, don't come crying to me

Which is best?

It *is* best to come crying to me

I'm good, when people come crying to me

I reform

I, I often cry too

It's not so bad

Don't feel sorry for me

Just be

And you don't

And it's not an emergency

It's not something that needs to be salved or bandaged

It's really okay

It is always there

Does that one

It is always there

Now, umh, I said that

It is always there, the program that supplies the information

that we don't

assimilate very easily

We are looking out the window, for example, and the stores have fabulous ***deals!!***

They're very expensive, but they're very fabulous!

You can just look out of one window into another window and you can tell

The sky's the limit!

In fact, most of them don't even have sky in them

Really special

Now you look up

You see more windows

and there the deals are very ambiguous

You have to kind of watch your choices there,

because anything could happen in those windows

It's

Skeptical people live there

They're thinking *too **hard***

about what might or might not be in it for *them*

And dark or light or sort of dark or sort of light

They have ***dimmers***

very advanced

They have dimmers that they can run by remote control from *Belize*

ENVY ENVY ENVY!!!!!

I want to control people remotely from Belize

and make them think that I'm going to sell them something that they

      can't have!!

But it's too late

I chose another path in life

Possibilities surround every instant

of theoretically sound reality crystal

Those two lines were all printed out in individual letters rather than written by script

You want me to read them again?

No I won't!

You heard them?

I'm sure

You got it

You got it

A fly is also in the room

Landing on the slanted ceiling

It did?

It stops buzzing, except when it bounds around for nothing

Another tomorrow fades into

decadence

Rise

Rice getting thrown

It's so different

It's different speaking from writing!

Writing is different from speaking!

Ahh, you already knew that
I have to come from home
and where I live we don't know anything
so
I'm in a strange place here
I'm doing my best
This is it
This is the beginning of the rest of it
It just started right there
where it said that
thing I just said
Uh, yeah, flies, flies in the room, right
These lines lengthen, skittering
away, across, what
That went really well
as they negotiate at cross purposes
their being written
Scampering
Scattering
They really do!!
They really do it
The fly is also in the room, right, I read that
Rice thrown at the windows!
It really says that, I think
No, rice thrown at new marrieds, simmers
Gradually the town surrounds the zoo
Then there's the part about possibilities site
Sip of tea
Maybe I can
Where is that?
If anybody wants to read along, you can read here
Really clever, very cute, all right
I don't think I can find it

Logic, I cannot respect anyway

I *like* that!!

Sounds reverberate in the space

People are toxic

Balloons are taking over, losing their helium power to a greater force

and, it, and it becomes, and in, it becomes incorporated, and so it's a person

and everything's all right again, back to the regular

This opportunity to leave an indelible trail!

Trial!

Although I love to walk and to be seen

for every momentary reflection is made testimony

in someone's mind

as they reflect

on the seeing

of me walking

for example, through Tomkins Square Park

or Union Square

or Times Square

Squared time

I don't seem to be living!!

It's a loop

Okay, so that means that we're at the beginning again of the loop

You weren't all listening when I said that before

I feel like a teacher, teaching college

I know poets are supposed to teach college but

it's not my thing

Like I said, I have clients, not students

I'm talking too much

I always talk too much!!

Ask my clients, they'll tell you

And the baby wailed blue murder

See if I would just, I don't know

You can talk too, it's really okay!

At the conference I was at, you know, it was really rude when people talked in
     loud voices while the speaker was speaking at the podium at the front in the
     grand ballroom and stuff like that, and you know, it's sort of
I would actually try *not* to turn around and look at them, because I didn't want to
     really make a point
I knew they'd stop, eventually
And the baby wailed blue murder
and the sky turned velvety black
and pigment froze in my skin
The message was over-complicated
The tiles shifted places on the floor erratically
This is so nice! It's like, you can join this
This is the best place in the room, really, if you're tired of the doorway
It's like the
It's like a sink, but it's so calm and nubbly at the same time, if you can imagine
You wouldn't regret it
though you'd be very close to *me!!*
But
Take your poison, you know?
Choose your poison
Choose
That's a better expression
seems kinder
I believe, we believe
I don't know, this is here again
I copied it twice
I work at a distance, sometimes across the room, sometimes by email, or phone
to bring things into focus
The words, the why not?
The donut
A question with an answer in it
You drink, and you feel your thirst
I believe, we be

I read that, tramp sails, yeah, okay

What!?!? What!?!?!? Are you calling me?!??!!!

I opened a second beer in the kitchen, keeping my balance with one hand on the island

I fail to wipe off the stove top, I wash the dishes and leave them in the drainer

Is that what you call it?

The plastic must be sprayed over the

muiihmiu

so it won't rust, so the dishes don't *scrape* noisily, so it's softer to touch

My hand used to drop things more often, when I wasn't sleeping enough

Okay

Um

We're getting toward the center of the reading, now

The center might be the heart, I'm not sure, let's see

that I was resting, loosing, losing, in my sleep

unable, waking, to recall, to me, last night, missing?, these lines

these lines!

Imagine a room, full of lines, in all directions

straight lines, all straight lines right now, please

And they

They're going all directions

three-dimensional, four-dimensional, five-dimensional, you name it!

Straight lines, can you imagine?!

It's like that times

What was that

Times plus?

Times square idea

Square times

The fifties

I haven't got

I was thinking I was going to say

Oh this is my Mad Men outfit, I got it at

But I couldn't remember what store they're selling them at so I didn't say that

Where does the sun

Nana Republic!

Grandma's Republic!

There should be such a store on every corner

I thought, yeah, like, right there

Rockefeller Center has turned into Banana Republic

Whoooahh!

That's my John Stewart routine

The ceiling was in the way, a white pink crust of sponged ridges, and snow
    covering the starlights

This isn't even the same part as the part about the tilted ceiling with the fly

This is a different part

Yeah, outside, no, I said that, no I didn't, and ridges, comma

and snow covering the skylights, outside, partly cloudy

So Stephen Ratliffe wrote one thousand pages, one a day, every day with the same
    rhyme scheme, no, with the same shape on the page, he put the commas in
    the same places pretty much, and he just did it looking out the window

Would you believe *that's how I wrote this too?!*

Huahgh?!

The ceiling was in the way, the skylights, outside, partly cloudy

Where *does* the sun set?

Everything passes in my lifetime

much of it recurring again and again in multiple directions

like the clouds

like the lines going through the room

like my intentions

like lines spoken in various plays one can imagine putting on with one's friends

It would be really fun!

Kind of—

You could do it anywhere

You could do it outside

in inclement weather, and, uh, because then you could use the umbrellas,
    and you could create special effects, with them

Like lines spoken in various plays, one I can ima

I, one, I, I can one, one can I, imagine

or make up out of tricks of memory seething, no, settling, tricks of memory settling

That's an interesting

locution

against a palpable horizon of consciousness

Deep!

You ain't heard nothing yet!

What comes next in history?

A lacuna, from our point of view

What do *we* know?

Ha-ha-ha!!!

FAKE-OUT!!

Doesn't say that

Because, we cannot possibly agree for long

After a brief blur of consensus

It sort of all joins together by syntax

That's one of the ways that it works

You can do it, too, if you want to

It's not as hard as you might think, but it's

It gets complicated the more you practice, that's the thing

If you only do it once every year or two, well, it seems really simple

but if you try it every day, every hour, if you just continuously do it for a while

it kind of grows on you, it affects you, it becomes part of you

and that's a very complicated place to, you know, uh, cultivate something

It's like, uh, what do they, what's a better word

unh! unh!

you know, like, ***germinate!***

No no no, it's not, it's uh, to

like the environment in which something grows, and it might be, you know, inside

of that thing, like supposing you had, uh, bacteria growing inside a potato, and

the potato's still *closed*, because the skin is all there, what would that be called?

There's a reason for it

But I forget the name

Everything passes in my lifetime

I'm processing it!

Unh, kind of between the lines, but

A lacuna, from our point of view

because we cannot possibly agree for long

After a brief war of consensus

joyful, or arrogant, or terrifying

consumes us all!

Okay, what consumes us all?

The thing that is

a lacuna?

Na-nuh-nah-ah-I-don't-know!

That sentence doesn't make too much sense

How do you feel about yourself, holding such a pessimistic world view?

Or is it

I got most of my deposit back, on the unbuilt house

but I don't know where it went.

The small print is leaking meaning in plots

as interpretation

We disgust

We revile ourselves

The words evaporate in our hearing

It's a very clean process

Hearing is very clean!

You're lucky!

I'm suffering!

The words evaporate in our hearing.

So simple!

Some people have a lot of *privilege!*

Against the context as a backdrop, I *plunge into* melodramatic oration!

It says here

This is really interesting

Ice

I lost my place

Itself, an enactment

Oh yeah, melodramatic oration, comma

itself an enactment of known qualifications

This is so weird, you know

I'm reading ahead, thinking

Is this going to be a good

Is this going to be a good line, or not?

Perverted, and loosed from judgment, in ironic spin

measure floating away

while the witness grimaces at difference

All one sentence

from about the ice, somewhere about there, on

So I am a very capable speaker

I'm not going to divest myself

of my authority to speak

until about eight o'clock

I . . live . . through . . words!

I wo-wo-wo-wo-wonder what I mean!

I wonder whether the meaning is

a storm or a sort of a dry

high barometric pressure area

or thundercloud or

pleasant day in, ah, New Jersey in the summer it's usually kind of humid

It's nice enough, if you're not in the smoggy parts

Harder to be sure you're heading forward

When you start at the top of the page, you don't necessarily know

about it

continuity, discontinuity

intentional, not intentional

It could be

your mind's playing tricks on you

or it could be you planned to come here to this

and it's all kind of shattering as you're here and you think

'cause this alternate possibility that it'll all hang together

'cause it's changing before your eyes focus

repeatedly

So, you know, you have to reestablish focus

You have to start over again, even though, you know, we're about two-thirds through

The harder to be sure you are heading forward

Time is different!

Time always heads forward

and that's why

you can kind of put your

You know time is a *fiction*

'cause that's not real

That's like sentence structure

You know, beginning, middle and end

It's not real

Don't kid yourself

These three trees in the middle of a wide avenue along the river

The cat leaps onto the high table while you watch from across the room

You know your shadow on the floor by its obvious direction

You know your shadow on the floor by its obvious direction

by its plain sympathy

by its color

There's a stain where candy leaked through the pants pocket

never washed out

so the student could not get to school

without everyone

wondering

something

they couldn't guess or understand

No words came

Disgust, dismay, disaffection, distance, disappearance

A big taste of amnesia and disaster

prone across the sidewalk onto the road

which was bumpy, hard, and unpleasantly covered with oil

Mmm!

Ohh!

Fatigue is unreasoning

Truth is impossible to establish

repeatedly

One time

you can make yourself an honorable mentioner of the truth

That's not the same as being a governor or a template for the truth

You don't have that privilege

I do

but *I misuse it, so it doesn't really matter!!*

You have a tremendous imagination, especially in the realm of forecasting the future

Despite being sociable

and easy to get along with

you may at times hurt others

because of your very independent and unconventional attitudes

If there's something new, you

go for it, *go* for it*, go for it!!*

I agree!

Okay

I want to do it right

I want to write it the way I do it

I want

I do what

I do want what I write

Ough!

um, or phone

to bring things into focus, the words, the why not, the donut!

the question with an answer in it

chess, Boggle, L Game

and feel your thirst

I believe, you believe. [Sneezes]

Feeling its comfortable, cloudy security under me, beneath the sheets,
    apprehensive actually to lie down, because I might fight with fate again
    tonight, against the grain, which presses back in the dark

Shivers

Wait

We gamble a moment on life

The cars skid around the arena

someone set up

without our knowledge

The cars skid around

Are we the elaboration of some I?

Reflection, the sense of, qualified

passed

to the

image

the endless image of fear

I'm not a

I'm sublime

I'm not against it

The consequences are rhyming with my negative imperative

Poetics term

The only umbrella in the house is shaped like a banana!

Are we the elaboration of some I

the sense of self-importance scarified and structured

by its implicit web

Be peace

Be

a relations to others

Relation to others!

Mama stumbled around the barroom

grabbing handfuls of peanuts and chips

desultorily whacking herself in between heavy forms vaguely resembling powder
    kegs and and and boulders in tee shirts and work pants saying nothing

Phwhuooh!

Here in a dark corner on the 31st floor

life seems to recede into cranky moods and dark woods

thinly embossed

and worked up into a semblance of perspective

and guilt

Zeal in serving

and a mild sense of urgency

aids *me* in maintaining stamina

while a yellow moon slides horizontally

across the ragged edge of treetops

glimpsed from my window

*How do I **do** it?*

Open my eyes and it's there

Open my eyes and it's there

Open my eyes and it's there

Image! Word! Word! Image! Image! Word! Word! Image!

People

People are images!

People may

You're very

very good at being quiet

But people do make words!

But usually

they just make their image and walk on

often not even

letting me know that they know that I'm here!

Someone is reading a text

allegedly written in a sort of code

without any prompts

besides an invitation to attempt it

all

a **life**

ostensibly

taken by its editor as an index of its culture

unmediated

though here with footnotes

curious what will get through

I mean, what will people understand?

They'll get an idea

from it, from it, from it, from it, from it somehow

as it closes the door magnetically

Myaaigghh!! It's a

It's a solid iron oak door

It's very expensive

and once it closes automatically, magnetically

it does not open for a thousand years

You're stuck in a fairy tale

Live with it!!

It no longer recognizes the adaptor

instead confirming its detection of new hardware

Is this the same door?

Little to say, but ever so much to figure out

I don't know what won't hurt me

so half-smile in admission of the entwinements of peace with aggression,

joy with suffering at color

BACKWARD

The four performance works documented in this book were each was built through advance planning and spontaneous decisions, in response to the opportunities and constraints I anticipated and experiences in the process of composition. Each depends on live improvisation to verbalize content, themes, and manner throughout the performance itself.

"Enter" is a transcript derived from a video recording of a public performance event arranged by the Poetry Center at San Francisco State University, inside the Unitarian Universalist Center on Nob Hill in San Francisco on the evening of May 31, 2005. I sat with my left side to the audience, facing an unfamiliar laptop I'd borrowed from Kit Robinson, as mine was unavailable.

The left column presents, verbatim, the words I spoke spontaneously into a microphone, amplified for those present during my oral improvisation. The right column presents, verbatim, the text that the audience saw me writing on the borrowed laptop, as it was projected on the concrete wall of the sanctuary they faced while I was typing it; several lines were visible at any one moment as the text scrolled above my head through its composition in progress.

My work was simultaneously spoken and written over a 35-minute period. Aside from the initial sentence, decided shortly beforehand, all the material was improvised, without advance decisions as to content or theme; I had decided in advance to perform repetitions and variations but not what they might say or how they should progress. Each line or utterance was intended to present an altered version of each previous, whether written or spoken.

An unexpected challenge arose as I began to type and speak. The laptop screen we had previously checked now remained black throughout the event, although the text written was successfully projected onto the concrete wall where the audience but not I could read it clearly.

In preparing the transcript, I eliminated punctuation marks, which all were commas, replacing them with three strikes on the space key. Blank lines in the left column may signify occasions where the voice was silent while more of the visible text appeared. Instances of line spaces in the right column represent moments when the voice was active while no writing was occurring at all.

"Transrelaflections" is another verbatim transcription of a performance, in this case the closing presentation for an academic conference on poetics, called "Authorship and the Turn to Language," organized by Barrett Watten, held December 1-4, 2005, at Universität Tübingen in Germany. Like the diverse papers over three preceding days, it occurred in the Fürstenzimmer, a large room on the second story of the ancient Schloß Hohentübingen above the old city center.

Bettina Fauser, a graduate student in the university, agreed to assist me by spontaneously speaking a few words in German about once a minute, translating a phrase or two I had just said in English, while we both moved about among chairs scattered in the negative space within a deep U formed of conference tables, at which participants and visitors sat.

I had brought a stack of file cards prepared on my flight, each with a word in German on one side and in English on the other, chosen by informal chance procedures from a German-English dictionary. Bettina passed these out to auditors during the event, and at moments I reached out to retrieve them from listeners and spoke in response to what I read. I also brought my laptop computer, preset at "pause" at a moment in Martin Scorsese's film *No Direction Home,* which I perched before the podium that faced the attendees. At my seat, I left my journal, from which I read a short passage at one point, and a scrap of paper on which I'd written a short list of phrases days earlier.

I kept this performance to twenty minutes, in accord with the university's demands to clear the room to prepare for another event that afternoon.

"Oration at Berkeley" was a 45-minute public improvised talk on March 19, 2009, in the Maud Fife Room at the University of California at Berkeley, commissioned as a concluding feature of "Medium & Margin: Multiplying Methodologies and Proliferating Poetics," a colloquium conference organized by Lyn Hejinian, Colin Dingler, and Mia You.

I brought my laptop to place at the lectern to one side of the raised space for performances and arranged in advance to project its screen's content very big onto the back wall or screen of that space. Since I understood this commission as a mandate for drawing out implications and creatively based reflections regarding the preceding days' presentations and discussions, I had attended each scheduled event and took notes during and after them, which I reviewed before my own performance. Some of these appeared on screen, as did some two-page spreads of contemporary poetry books and a slide show showing people descending an escalator. I also ran some ambient sound recorded on preceding days, to be heard behind my live speaking voice at times.

As well as helping set up tech for this event, Konrad Steiner recorded it on a video that can currently be seen at https://media.sas.upenn.edu/app/public/watch.php?file_id=86970, approachable through the Steve Benson author's page at Pennsound.

"Time Squared" represents a one-hour reading performance I was asked to give at the Emily Harvey Foundation in a loft in SoHo, New York City, on the evening of March 2, 2012.

There was a low intensity area light in the central zone of the space, around which people stood or sat, with just a few chairs. A microphone was suspended from the ceiling. Gradually I became aware of ice cubes someone had affixed up there too, dripping or falling occasionally. My text, several photocopied pages from a long hand-written poem I had been writing late each evening, lay on a shaggy area rug someone had left in the center of the space.

I had placed three boom boxes at different areas around the center zone, all set to play the same recording of my reading at home from the written materials on the floor. At 7 o'clock, the time announced for my work, I began to speak, without looking at any paper, while the chatter of the audience at first made me hard to hear. I turned the boom boxes on at this point, one after another, and regulated their volume occasionally during the following 60 minutes as they played out of synch. Often only faintly audible, these voicings are not included in the transcript. At times, I read from the pages on the floor, often altering the texts as I read them.

The audio recording I had arranged with the gallery to have made ran out for some reason after 47 minutes. A planned video recording never appeared.

I made all these transcripts at home in Maine, in months following the events recorded.

DATES AND SITES OF PERFORMANCES
COLLECTED IN THIS BOOK

"Enter," May 31, 2005, Unitarian Universalist Center, Nob Hill, San Francisco, by arrangement with the Poetry Center at San Francisco State University.

"Transrelaflections," December 4, 2005, in the Fürstenzimmer of die Schloss, Universität Tubingen, Tübingen, Germany.

"Oration at Berkeley," March 19, 2009, The Maud Fife Room, University of California at Berkeley.

"Time Squared," March 2, 2012, The Emily Harvey Foundation, New York, New York.

THE UNPREDICTABLE NOW:
SOME NOTES ON MY IMPROVISATIONAL WORK

Each time I planned such a performance, I wanted and intended not to do anything perfectly or better than others would, if indeed others would ever attempt such stunts, but to do my very best in generating the work. But—best at what? How would I assess what's best? The terms for "my best" were usually vague and nonverbal. The skills and imaginative play and wisdom entailed might vary over time and within any one work. A choice to allow such indeterminate variance could be a strength of the work, or at least an aspect of its distinct, non-standardized game plan. I've never sought to recruit someone to direct or improve my practice in all of this.

Generalizing among different presentations I've undertaken as performance works may be invalid. I haven't aimed for developing consistency or progress in this sort of work. I'm skeptical whether readers of this book will find support or use in notes I can make about my method in general, but I am wishful myself of a description of some of the typical factors among the works I've made in this way, without attempting to establish any theoretical framework or validation.

Since around 1977, whenever I have accepted an invitation to do a poetry reading, I haven't yet known what I would do when the time came to present work. I may have thought of recent work I'd like to read aloud, but if a variation or an alternative idea occurred to me as interesting or compelling for making something through the ways I would speak or read in the actual event, I might choose to follow that lead.

Although on rare occasions I have simply spoken gibberish or silently enacted an imagined sequence of activities, usually my improvised work has depended on voicing in English some of the words and ideas that crossed my mind at the time of performing. My design for any one piece consisted mainly of further conditions and constraints: how many minutes long it would be, how it would complement the audience expectations and the physical and institutional space of its performance, how much I might move around in space, and how I might make use of auxiliary technology and devices, such as microphone and amplifier, pre-recorded environmental sounds, lighting, projections of film or photos, physical props, and my personal laptop.

Any decisions I set for myself in advance became constraints on the performance to be observed or violated. My experiment and practice with them before the event might be anything from extensive to nil. Unpredictable choices sometimes arose as a consequence of technical or creative confusions or dysfunctions, which immediately became factors in the development of that work.

I've liked going second if on a double bill, whether reading or improvising, because attending to the other writer's presentation seemed to raise my own impetus to generate an energetic and disruptive performance. After presenting, I often find it embarrassingly hard to listen attentively to someone else's work.

Optimally, a quality of reverie would underlie every passage within the improvisation. I usually wanted to handle the occasion confidently, playfully, sincerely, but I learned that I couldn't count on maintaining such an attitude, even as a style or role. Sometimes I spoke on issues or positions I took seriously or felt as consequential, even if I had not intended to sustain any themes at all.

Under the stress of responsibility to those who were present (the audience, my hosts, and myself), I couldn't always keep up a relaxed, easy-going, fluent, free-spirited manner throughout the piece. If I began to doubt the value or vitality of what I was saying, I might tense up. Sometimes this led to a repetitious, stuck sequence of verbal passages or an overly abstract and aimless elaboration of no certain concept, compounding my suspicion that no one was feeling engaged, moved, or amused.

If I blocked or felt seized up this way, I might hope to remember and try one or two tricks of language use to set up alternative openings. These might include arbitrarily changing up the verb tenses or pronouns, violating conventional sentence structure, changing the subject, lying unreasonably about anything, stopping and starting abruptly, barking, shifting syntax or context of utterance radically, drawing on some vocabulary inappropriate to the occasion or issue being referenced, or otherwise screwing with whatever I might have thought or meant to say.

I meant my oral delivery to be clear, so I tried to know what each word would be in advance of vocalizing it. So, sometimes I paused between words or phrases, indecisive or failing to think of alternatives that engaged me. In such momentary gaps, audience members might empathize with my apparent strain, anxiety, or helplessness, or they might silently conceive any words that they thought could come next.

I try to be guided by my curiosity and to accept all my uncertainties as a given. Not knowing and not yet understanding have seemed like core principles in this sort of work. My process seems driven and oriented by a dialectical give-and-take or conversation between a seeming knowledge and my apparent not knowing. Usually, afterward, I can't remember much of what I said or felt or thought during the performance, especially when I've sensed overall that it had gone well.

Typically, I come to the occasion itself with preconceived, set decisions about how I would speak, and any limits I'd have set on it, and no structural or thematic design beyond that. What's valuable and what to take away from the piece remain up to the listener. Readers of this book may choose to suspend some values and expectations, to discover what others occur to them through reading. I often have made a verbatim transcription afterward, to find out for myself how I can learn from the work. Some of these transcriptions I have been glad to publish in print, where they may occupy a gray zone between literature and documentation.

January 23, 2025

ACKNOWLEDGMENTS

Thanks to those whose support and invitation gave these works occasion to be made, including The Poetry Center at San Francisco State University, Barrett Watten and the Universität Tübingen, Lyn Hejinian, Mia You, and Carol Dingler at the University of California at Berkeley, and the Emily Harvey Foundation in New York City.

I am grateful also to those who published these works years ago in magazines, including Cecilia Wu of *critiphoria* online, Michael Friedman of *Shiny Magazine*, and Louis Armand of *Vlak*.

I warmly thank all those who helped with technical and contextual arrangements, including Kit Robinson, Steve Dickerson, Bettina Fauser, Barrett Watten, and Konrad Steiner. The processes through which these events came into being would have been impossible without their willing contributions and confidence.

I am especially grateful to David Wilk at City Point Press for inviting a manuscript and accepting this peculiarly challenging project. He has supported and organized its publication with skill, assurance, and grace. Thanks too for the outstanding work of designer and typesetter HR Hegnauer, who brilliantly handled the complexities and challenges of bringing these works into print.

STEVE BENSON

Steve Benson was born in 1949 and grew up in central New Jersey. He studied for degrees at Yale College, University of California at Irvine, and The Wright Institute. From 1976 until 1992 he lived in the San Francisco Bay Area, working in new and used book and music retail while building friendships and raising questions with fellow language-centered writers in their frequent contacts. His public readings often incorporated collaboration, auxiliary media, oral improvisation, fortuitous resolutions to unanticipated technical problems, and collaboration with writers, musicians, and filmmakers.

He acted in Carla Harryman's *Third Man* and Alan Bernheimer's *Particle Arms* for Poets Theater productions in the 1980s. He directed a performance of Harryman's play *La Quotidienne* in 1983 and a poets theater workshop at Intersection for the Arts in 1992. Previous books of his performance transcripts and other writings are *Blindspots* (Whale Cloth, 1981), *Blue Book* (The Figures/Roof, 1988), *Reverse Order* (Potes & Poets, 1989), *Open Clothes* (Atelos, 2005), and *It's a Stool Pigeon Universe* (Rastacan, 2021). Other poetry books include *Briarcombe Paragraphs* (Moving Letters, 1985), *Roaring Spring* (Zasterle, 1998), and *As It Happens* (Lulu, 2021). He collaborated with nine friends in language poetry to prepare *The Grand Piano: An experiment in collaborative autobiography* (Mode A, 2006-10) and, in collaboration with Suzanne Stein, in 36 improvised public on-line chat messaging performances, now collected in *Do Your Own Damn Laundry* (Gauss.pdf, 2019).

Steve has lived in Surry, Maine, since 1996, serving the Hancock Peninsula as a psychologist in private practice until 2024. He has gratefully shared parenting two children to adulthood with his former spouse. He is an active member of Morgan Bay Zendo, Climate Psychology Alliance, and USA-Palestine Mental Health Network, among other organizations. Links to his works online are to be found at http://www.stevebensonasis.com. Pennsound maintains accessible audio and visual recordings of numerous readings and performances.

PREVIOUS BOOKS

As Is, 1978, The Figures, Berkeley, California

The Busses, 1981, Tuumba, Berkeley, California

Blindspots, 1981, Whale Cloth, Cambridge, Massachusetts

Dominance, 1985, The Coincidence, Oakland, California

Briarcombe Paragraphs, 1985, Moving Letters, Paris, France.

Blue Book, 1988, The Figures, Great Barrington, Massachusetts, and Roof, New York, New York.

Reverse Order, 1988, Potes and Poets, Elmwood, Connecticut.

Roaring Spring, 1988, Zasterle, Tenerife, Canary Islands, Spain.

Open Clothes, 2005, Atelos, Berkeley, California.

The Grand Piano: An Experiment in Collective Autobiography, in ten volumes, written in collaboration with Rae Armantrout, Carla Harryman, Tom Mandel, Ted Pearson, Bob Perelman, Kit Robinson, Ron Silliman, and Barrett Watten, 2010, Mode A, Detroit, Michigan.

Do Your Own Damn Laundry, written in collaboration with Suzanne Stein, 2019, Gauss.pdf, online.

As It Happens, 2021, self-published with Lulu, online.

It's a Stool Pigeon Universe, 2021, Rastacan, online.